Thin-Section Petrography
of
Ceramic Materials

INSTAP ARCHAEOLOGICAL EXCAVATION MANUAL 2

Thin-Section Petrography
of
Ceramic Materials

INSTAP ARCHAEOLOGICAL EXCAVATION MANUAL 2

by

Sarah E. Peterson

with contributions by

Philip P. Betancourt

Published by
INSTAP Academic Press
Philadelphia, Pennsylvania
2009

Design and Production
INSTAP Academic Press
Philadelphia, PA, USA

Printing and Binding
CRWGraphics
Pennsauken, NJ, USA

Cover photo after Day and Relaki 2003, pl. 2C, sample no. 95/62.

Library of Congress Cataloging-in-Publication Data

Peterson, Sarah E., 1983-
 Thin-section petrography of ceramic materials / by Sarah E. Peterson ; with contributions by Philip P. Betancourt
        p. cm. -- (INSTAP archaeological excavation manual ; v. 2)
 Includes bibliographical references.
 ISBN 978-1-931534-55-0 (alk. paper)
 1. Petrology in archaeology. 2. Ceramics--Analysis. I. Betancourt, Philip P., 1936- II. Title.
CC79.P4P46 2009
552'.06--dc22

                                                                2009017409

Contents

List of Figures

Introduction

Thin-section petrography is a useful methodology for the study and classification of clay fabrics. Thin sections can be used to examine a wide variety of materials, including rocks, minerals, slags, concrete, mudbrick, and plaster, as well as fired clays. The method can provide evidence for a number of important aspects of ceramic studies including the determination of provenance and the reconstruction of technology.

A thin section is created by sawing off a small fragment of the material to be studied, attaching the resulting flat surface to a glass microscope slide, and grinding the exposed surface of the fragment down to a standard thickness (ca. 25–30 micrometers) (Fig. 1). The thin section is then examined using a polarizing microscope (Fig. 2). At the standard thickness, the mineral inclusions present in the fabric become transparent and can be identified based on characteristic optical properties (Bambauer, Taborszky, and Trochim 1979; Deer, Howie, and Zussman 1996; Nesse 2004). The fabric can then be classified through the identification and examination of its plastic and aplastic components, microstructure, and texture.

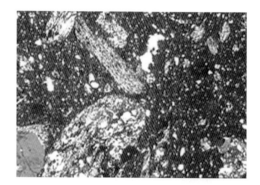

Figure 1. *Photomicrograph of a thin section of a coarse vessel from Mochlos in cross-polarized light showing large, weathered phyllite inclusions (after Day and Relaki 2003, pl. 1A, sample no. 95/50). Horizontal dimension = 4 mm.*

Figure 2. *Eleni Nodarou using a petrographic microscope to study thin sections of pottery at the Institute for Aegean Prehistory Study Center for East Crete, Pacheia Ammos, Crete, Greece. Photo by Chronis Papanikolopoulos.*

Goals for the Thin-Section Petrography of Ceramics

In modern studies concerning ancient pottery, archaeological ceramics are studied for the information they provide on many subjects including technology, style, functions, chronology, place of origin, and symbolic content. All vessels, including plain storage and transport containers as well as fine vases for serving and display, contribute essential data toward the understanding of past cultures. Ceramic petrography is one of the indispensible analytical techniques for modern ceramic studies. It characterizes the fabric of clay materials through its microscopic examination in thin-section. Different fabrics and their characteristics can be distinguished based on various details of the microstructure that cannot be seen or readily identified by the naked eye or through low-level magnification, enabling researchers to detect details that might otherwise be overlooked or misinterpreted with traditional macroscopic methods.

Many of the features of a ceramic fabric can be observed in thin section:

1. Nature and characteristics of non-plastic inclusions (mineralogical composition and the relative percentage, size, shape, distribution, and orientation of different particles)

2. Textural and optical characteristics of the clay matrix (such as birefringence and color)

3. Shape, quantity, and orientation of voids

4. Relationship between the body of the ceramic material and the surface/decoration

The interpretation of these features allows a researcher to better accomplish the goal of understanding the past. Petrography contributes information on the character of a ceramic fabric and the materials used to create it as well as on the choices that craftsmen made during the process of refining the clay, forming the vessel, and firing it to create a more permanent product. By establishing similarities and differences between fabrics, one can determine relationships between different wares, identify characteristics that indicate provenance, and reconstruct technological processes involved in manufacturing (including selection and treatment of raw materials, forming techniques, decorative systems, and firing characteristics). Understanding the nature of these processes can make important contributions to our knowledge of the past, especially in regard to sources of raw materials, spatial distribution of traded goods, specialization of manufacturing techniques, and the development of technology.

History of Thin-Section Petrography

FOUNDATION OF THE METHOD

Scottish scientist William Nicol created the first thin sections during the later part of the 18th century, producing samples of fossilized wood that were thin enough to be transparent under a microscope. He then examined the sections to determine the species of tree from which they originated (Sorby 1882, 101; Humphries 1992, 2; Croft 2006, 20, 33). Nicol also contributed to the creation of the first polarizing microscope in 1828 by inventing a prism that enabled the transmission of a single beam of plane-polarized light. Two of these "Nicol" prisms were first applied to a microscope in 1834 by Englishman William Henry Fox Talbot (Humphries 1992, 2; Croft 2006, 18–20). Following this innovation, some of the first objects to be examined were thin sections of wood, fossils, minerals, and teeth (Humphries 1992, 2).

Henry Clifton Sorby, an English scientist affiliated with Sheffield University, was the first to demonstrate that the characteristic optical properties exhibited by minerals in polarized light enables their identification (Humphries 1992, 2). Sorby was aware of the practice of examining thin sections of fossils and teeth under a microscope, and in 1849 he created the first thin sections of rocks from carbon- iferous limestone in Derbyshire (Sorby 1882, 102; Humphries 1992, 2). He fash- ioned his sections by grinding thin samples on sandstone slabs with emery powder and water and then attaching the completed specimens to glass slides (Sorby 1882, 103–106, 133–134; Humphries 1992, 2–3). In 1851, Sorby published the first description of the mineral composition of a rock following a study of limestone from the Yorkshire coast (Sorby 1851). Through the analysis of thin sections of the limestone in polarized light, he differentiated between inclusions of agate and calcite based on characteristics such as color, shape, and birefringence. Sorby pub- lished a full description of his thin-sectioning methods in 1882, and his techniques became standard in the fields of geology, petrology, and sedimentology.

One of the first studies that utilized thin-sectioning techniques for the analysis of archaeological materials was published in 1890 by German geologist Karl Georg Richard Lepsius. Funded by the Royal Prussian Academy of Science, Lepsius traveled to Greece in 1887 and 1889 in order to produce a geological map of the Attica region (Moltesen 1994, 7, 15–16). During his visits, Lepsius obtained 409 marble samples from Classical sculptures and quarries. He prepared thin sections of the collected samples and classified different types of marble on the basis of microscopically observed details such as color and grain size of inclusions (Lepsius 1890). The criteria that Lepsius developed for his categorizations were widely used by Classical archaeologists for the study of marble, but the re-examination of many of his samples with modern techniques has proven them to be unreliable (Moltesen 1994, 16–19).

THIN-SECTION PETROGRAPHY OF CERAMIC MATERIALS

An analysis of some significant investigations that have been undertaken specifically on ceramic materials demonstrates some of the different types of archaeological problems that can be addressed through thin-section analysis. The utilization of the method explicitly for the study of ceramics was not widely realized until the work of Anna O. Shepard in the 20th century. In 1942, she published the results of a large-scale petrographic analysis of Rio Grande Glaze Paint pottery, which comes from the area of Pecos, New Mexico, a site occupied between 1300 A.D. and 1838 A.D. (Shepard 1965, 65). Through the analysis of the technology of the pottery fabrics, Shepard was able to obtain information that stylistic and morphological analyses could not provide. She identified several different types of wares on the basis of distinct temper inclusions visible in thin section, and she also examined the geology of the region in order to obtain information about raw material sources. Shepard subsequently determined that the tempering material present in much of the sampled pottery would not have been available to local potters at Pecos. She therefore concluded that a significant amount was imported from elsewhere and thus provided evidence for the existence of large-scale trade networks and craft specialization in the region (Shepard 1942; 1965, 66, 68–71). Shepard further highlighted the importance of the study of ceramic technology and the value of petrographic analysis in her volume *Ceramics for the Archaeologist* (1956, 1–5, 139, 157–159).

Nearly parallel to Shepard's work in the Americas, Wayne M. Felts at the University of Cincinnati was carrying out a petrographic analysis of pottery and soil samples taken from Troy on the western coast of Turkey (Felts 1942). Felts was similarly able to demonstrate the value of petrography to the understanding of ancient ceramic technology through the examination of ceramic fabrics in thin section. He compared the geology of the tempering materials in the pottery from Troy to that of the soil samples and used the resulting data to differentiate between local and imported wares. Additional analysis of the internal characteristics of the fabrics revealed that the imported pottery often had different firing and forming techniques than those of local origin. Furthermore, because the study involved pottery collected from several different layers and locations during excavation, Felts identified differences in fabric composition and forming processes over time and space (Felts 1942).

The importance of technology to the study of ancient pottery was emphasized further by the work of Frederick R. Matson. In 1942, Matson published an article titled "Technological Ceramic Studies," in which he submitted that morphological and stylistic analyses of pottery alone were not sufficient to the understanding of ancient cultures. He argued that researchers must analyze the technological processes and raw materials involved in the creation of ceramic materials in order to understand the role of the potter and his or her products in society. Matson advocated the use of thin-section analysis for this purpose and also extolled the value of collecting and studying samples of local clays and tempering materials (Matson 1942, 26–27). His theoretical ideas eventually came together in the concept of ceramic ecology, a multi-disciplinary approach that aimed to better understand the influence of culture on the creation of ceramic materials (Matson 1965). Matson employed techniques relating to ceramic ecology in his study of pottery collections from excavations carried out in the Amuq Valley, Turkey, by the Syrian Expedition of the Oriental Institute of the University of Chicago. In 1945, he published a summary of the technological development of pottery in the region during the Chalcolithic Age, and a more detailed analysis of his results was published in 1960 as part of a comprehensive volume on the excavations (Matson 1945; Braidwood and Braidwood 1960, 31–35, 42). Matson studied 308 sherds from the Amuq Valley in thin section, classified different fabric types according to their mineralogy, and traced developments in raw material selection and treatment over time. He also obtained clay samples from areas in the region and similarly analyzed them on the basis of mineral content in order to differentiate between local and imported materials. Later, he was involved in the Minnesota Messenia Expedition in Greece, wherein he supplemented the petrographic analysis of collected pottery sherds with an ethnographic study of modern production throughout the region (Matson 1972, 200–224).

Ceramic petrography became increasingly popular, particularly in Europe, following the work of David Peacock in Britain. In 1968, Peacock published the results of the study of approximately 100 thin sections of two Iron Age wares from the Herefordshire-Cotswold region in western England. Previous research had classified the first ware, Western Second B, as an indigenous product and considered the second, Western Third B, representative of an intrusive culture. Peacock determined, however, that fabrics of both wares contained lithic temper inclusions compatible with the geology of the nearby Malvern Hills. He therefore concluded that both Western Second B and Western Third B pottery were made locally with the same materials and suggested that variations in style could be attributed to the presence of different production centers operating and trading throughout the region (Peacock 1968). In a later petrographic study of coarse Roman pottery from Fishbourne, England, Peacock utilized textural analysis to aid in the classification of pottery, the methods of which are derived from sedimentary petrology (Peacock 1971). Three different pottery groups were analyzed in thin section, including sandy wares that contained significant quantities of quartz minerals. Because quartz minerals are a common component of most soils, their recognition as inclusions are often of little use for the distinction of ceramic fabrics. By employing textural analysis, however, Peacock could discern characteristic differences between quartz inclusions, such as the roundness, sphericity, percentage, and size distribution of individual grains. He therefore was able to differentiate between ceramic fabrics on the basis of texture and determine whether or not the raw material inclusions present in the sandy wares from Fishbourne were derived from the same source (Peacock 1971). Although he was not the first to employ textural analysis in petrography, Peacock's studies demonstrated the value of the technique to the characterization of pottery in thin section and contributed significantly to its popularization.

In the Aegean, the value of petrographic analysis has been demonstrated by a number of important investigations. For example, H.-C. Einfalt of Karlsruhe University performed both petrographic and chemical analyses on a small number of sherds and clayish rocks from Akrotiri, Thera, and determined that although there are no clay deposits suitable for large scale production on the island, a large number of the samples were manufactured there from local materials (Einfalt 1979). A similar examination, involving only thin-section analysis, was performed on Late Bronze Age Theran pottery by David F. Williams of the University of Southampton in order to describe and classify locally produced fabrics and enable the recognition of imported wares (Williams 1979b). W. Noll also performed thin-section and other analyses on an assemblage of pottery sherds from Akrotiri and compared the samples to Late Minoan I Kamares Ware to facilitate the under-standing of similarities in manufacturing techniques (Noll 1979).

During the same period, J.A. Riley studied Roman and Islamic materials from Cyrenaica in Libya and was able to characterize the geology of relevant areas with the region in addition to performing a petrological examination of the ceramics (Riley 1979). Additionally, George H. Myer's work on Vasiliki Ware, part of the multi-disciplinary Philadelphia Vasiliki Ware Project carried out under the direction of Philip P. Betancourt, revealed the contributions that petrography can make to the study of specific ware groups (Betancourt et al. 1979; Myer and Betancourt 1981). Soon after, Myer was also involved in a comprehensive examination of East Cretan White-on-Dark Ware (Betancourt 1984). Riley also performed petrographic analyses on ceramic materials from Crete and mainland Greece, which revealed patterns in exchange and variations in raw material selection over time (Riley, Peacock, and Renfrew 1980; Riley 1981a; 1981c; 1982; 1983). Furthermore, Riley studied Bronze Age ceramic materials from the area of the Qoueiq River in northern Syria in association with the Tell Rifa'at Survey, which took place from 1977–1979 (Riley 1981b; 1981d). Ian K. Whitbread of the University of Leicester made further contributions, advocating the use of techniques that were developed for soil micromorphology to describe the microstructure of ceramic fabrics in thin section, thereby enabling more accurate and detailed characterizations (Whitbread 1986, 1989). Also, a useful review of the scientific analyses performed on a wide range of Greek and Cypriot pottery was published by R.E. Jones in 1986, which demonstrated the usefulness of thin-section analysis and other forms of examination (Jones 1986).

In the next decade, Sarah J. Vaughan carried out significant analyses in Cyprus and the Cyclades, which served as examples of comprehensive petrographic studies and helped to form more accurate criteria for the classification and sourcing of ceramic materials (Vaughan 1990, 1991a, 1991b). George H. Myer also continued his research in the 1990s, lending his expertise to a number of investigations focused on pottery production at individual sites (Myer and Betancourt 1990; Myer, McIntosh, and Betancourt 1995). Other important investigations have been carried out by Peter M. Day of Sheffield University, whose analyses have enhanced the understanding of regional and local production and distribution practices and demonstrated the potential of combining thin-section petrography with chemical analyses and scanning electron microscopy (Day 1995, 1997; Day, Wilson, and Kiriatzi 1997; Day and Wilson 1998; Day et al. 1999; Day and Kilkoglou 2001, 115). Additionally, the work of Christine Shriner of Indiana University on pottery from Lerna significantly highlighted the need for researchers to supplement fabric analyses with the study of local raw material sources to aid in the determination of provenance (Shriner and Dorais 1999; Shriner and Murray 2001). By the beginning of the 21st century, ceramic petrography was becoming an essential component of modern pottery studies, especially those dealing with Aegean prehistory. Full-time positions in the field had been established at several institutions, and the inclusion of thin-section analysis was considered a routine component for integrated studies of archaeological pottery.

Preparation of Thin Sections

A ceramic thin section is created by first cutting a small fragment from the sample using a non-deformational diamond saw (Fig. 3). If the material is extremely porous or friable, it may be impregnated with resin before sectioning to ensure that it will not become damaged. The sawn surface is then ground, either by hand or with a grinding machine, until it is completely flat, and it is attached to a glass slide with an epoxy or mounting medium (Fig. 4). When the medium has dried, the top of the sample that is parallel to the slide is cut down to a thickness of 1–2 mm. This newly cut surface is similarly ground with fine abrasives until it is between 25 and 30 micrometers thick. A glass cover slip is then mounted over the thin section for protection, or alternatively the surface of the section is polished. Following this process, researchers are left with the object from which the sample was taken, fragments that have been cut during preparation, and the completed thin section, all of which are valuable reference materials. Completed thin sections and fragments can be archived in a petrographic library or other facility to aid future research.

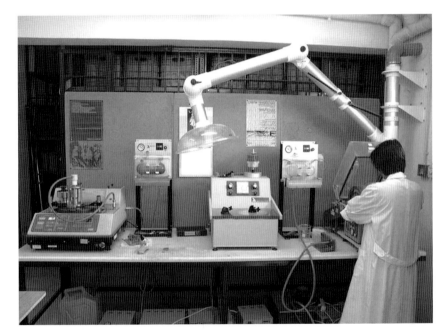

Figure 3. Eleni Nodarou using a non-deformational diamond saw in the William A. McDonald Petrography Laboratory at the Institute for Aegean Prehistory Study Center for East Crete, Pacheia Ammos, Crete, Greece. Photo by Elizabeth Shank.

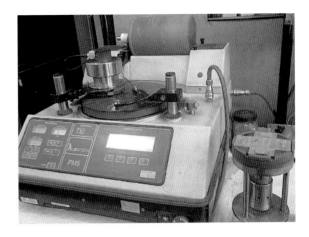

Figure 4. *Lapping machine used to grind thin sections to a desired thickness. Photo by Eleanor Huffman.*

Examination and Analysis of Thin Sections

The main goal of ceramic petrography is the characterization of the fabric of materials made of clay through the examination of thin sections. This task is accomplished primarily with the aid of the polarizing microscope (Fig. 2). This type of microscope transmits polarized light through mounted thin sections, allowing for the identification of two main components, the clay matrix and non-plastic inclusions. In addition, one can examine pores and voids, as well as observe details about surface treatment. The appearance and the technical properties of the final product are determined by the type, abundance, and characteristics of these features, and through their identification and analysis within a thin section, the fabric of the ceramic material can be characterized and information about production technology and provenance can be obtained. In addition to the observation of the qualitative properties of the fabric, it is also possible to attain useful quantitative data through statistical and digital imaging analyses.

NON-PLASTIC INCLUSIONS

The majority of petrographic thin-section analyses are focused mainly on the characterization of non-plastic inclusions. These inclusions, often called the coarse fraction of the ceramic fabric, are frequently present in naturally occurring clay deposits. They can also be intentionally added to clays to reduce the plasticity of the ceramic paste, enhance its workability, reduce adverse effects of shrinkage and expansion, increase thermal resistance during firing, and strengthen the body of the final product (Williams 1979b, 74). Several types of non-plastic materials can be identified in thin sections:

1. Mineral inclusions or rock fragments (Figs. 1, 5)

2. Organic inclusions (such as plant materials, shells, and bones; Fig. 6)

3. Grog (crushed fragments of previously fired ceramics)

Minerals are the most common and easiest to classify of the non-plastic inclusions found in clay fabrics. They are identified by characteristic optical properties displayed under plane-polarized light and crossed polars, including transparency, color, pleochroism, morphology, birefringence, and isotropism or anisotropism. Within inclusions of submarine basalt, for example, it is possible to observe characteristic straw-shaped mineral formations that are indicative of underwater formation (Fig. 7). Several sources exist to aid in the analysis and classification of minerals in thin sections; some standard references are H.U. Bambauer, F. Taborszky, and H.D. Trochim's *Optical Determination of Rock-Forming Minerals* (1979), W.A. Deer, R.A. Howie, J. Zussman's *An Introduction to Rock-Forming Minerals* (1996), and W.D. Nesse's *Introduction to Optical Mineralogy* (2004).

It is sometimes possible to differentiate between natural inclusions and added temper; the latter may be discernable based on abundance, composition, size, shape, and distribution throughout the ceramic fabric, depending on the potter's treatment of the material prior to its addition to the paste. Non-plastic inclusions may be ground or crushed to obtain a necessary size or texture, mixed with other raw materials, or processed through decantation or separation (Shepard 1956,

Figure 5. *Photomicrograph of a thin section of a vessel from Mochlos, Crete, in cross-polarized light. It features large, angular calcite and dolomite inclusions (after Day and Relaki 2003, pl. 2C, sample no. 95/62). Horizontal dimension = 4 mm.*

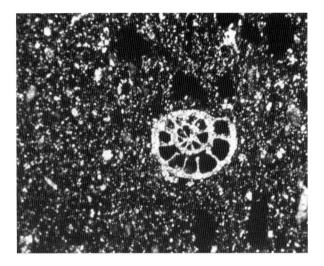

Figure 6. *Photomicrograph of a thin section of a vessel from Kommos, Crete, displaying a microfossil inclusion within the fabric (after Myer and Betancourt 1990, pl. A, sample no. T 111). Width of field = 1.2 mm.*

Figure 7. *Photomicrograph of a thin section of a vessel from Kommos, Crete, displaying characteristic "soda straw" plagioclase crystals within a particle of basalt (after Myer and Betancourt 1990, pl. A, sample no. T 190). Width of field = 0.8 mm.*

117; Reedy 2008, 131, 151). The large phyllite inclusions visible in Figure 1, for example, are rounded, an indication that they were weathered prior to their inclusion in the ceramic paste. Therefore, the non-plastic inclusions present in this fabric were either a naturally occurring component of the clay source or were not processed prior to their addition to the fabric. By contrast, the large, angular qualities of the calcite and dolomite inclusions present in Figure 5 signify that these inclusions were likely crushed or ground prior to their intentional addition to the paste. Grog tempers will also commonly exhibit angular properties when observed in thin section, and many organic tempers burn out of the clay fabric during firing and can be identified by the appearance of carbonized (black) spots or by voids or vugs left behind (Whitbread 1986, 82; Orton, Tyers, and Vince 1993, 133–135; Velde and Druc 1999, 142–144; Reedy 2008, 184–189).

The minerals in a ceramic fabric can often provide general information about firing as changes in mineralogy can occur when certain temperatures are reached, although these alterations are more often detected with x-ray diffraction, infrared spectroscopy, and other methods rather than through thin-section analysis (Reedy 2008, 184–185). The understanding of firing conditions can be complicated, however, as other factors such as the rate of the rise in temperature or the atmospheric conditions during the process will also affect the properties of the fabric (Orton, Tyers, and Vince 1993, 133–135; Velde and Druc 1999, 96–104; Reedy 2008, 184).

The forming technique utilized in the production of a ceramic material can sometimes be ascertained through the analysis of non-plastic inclusions in thin section, as the method utilized during the forming of a clay paste into a desired shape will align non-plastic inclusions in characteristic ways. When pottery is wheel-thrown, for example, particles will be arranged parallel to the rim and base of the vessel. Other types of alignment observed in thin section will be indicative of other forming techniques, and the arrangement of inclusions is also dependant on the orientation of the section taken for analysis (Shepard 1956, 183–186; Woods 1985; Whitbread 1996; Roux and Courty 1998; Reedy 2008, 180–184). It is important to note, however, that any combination of forming methods may be utilized in the construction of a ceramic material, a detail that can cause difficulties in interpretation.

In some instances, it is possible to identify the specific geologic source for the non-plastic inclusions present in ceramic fabrics. During petrographic analysis, the sourcing of raw materials requires researchers to have knowledge of the geology in the area surrounding the archaeological site, and it is advisable to carry out the systematic collection and analysis of potential source materials for comparison and then fire those materials in a kiln if reference samples do not exist. Information about raw material sources can provide insight into a number of archaeological issues, including local production and distribution practices, changes over time in the selection and treatment of raw materials, and trade and exchange patterns. Knowledge of what materials potters utilized in the production of ceramics can sometimes enable researchers to identify different workshops or production areas.

In regions where the geology is homogenous, however, it may be impossible to locate the original source of tempering materials. This task is further complicated when potters mix clays and tempering materials from a number of sources or when these materials are imported from other regions (Williams 1979a, 74–75; Orton, Tyers, and Vince 1993, 135; Reedy 2008, 151, 164–165).

CLAY MATRIX

The clay matrix is the most abundant substance found in clay fabrics, and it is made of clay minerals and other materials whose grain-size is less than 2 micrometers in diameter (Velde and Druc 1999, 5, 35). The non-clay minerals present in the clay matrix, like other non-plastic inclusions, may occur naturally or may be intentionally added. Clay minerals are the component of the ceramic paste that enables its plasticity, because the thin, sheet-like shapes of aggregations of clay minerals serve to attract water to their surfaces, thereby permitting them to easily slide over one another and facilitate the molding of the clay paste (Velde and Druc 1999, 36–38, 56). Clay minerals make up the majority of the clay fabric, but because of their microscopic size, most are impossible to identify through thin-section analysis (Reedy 2008, 124). However, techniques have been developed for the general characterization of the clay matrix that rely primarily on optical properties, such as birefringence, anisotropy, or isotropy.

It is sometimes possible to determine the way in which a ceramic material was fired through the observation of the color or birefringence of the clay matrix in thin section. In high temperatures, the clay minerals in the matrix are vitrified and sintered, forming spinel and glass, thereby giving the matrix an isotropic appearance. Furthermore, a ceramic fabric that exhibits different layers of color within its matrix can provide information about raw material inclusions and firing conditions (Reedy 2008, 185). Additionally, the alignment of clay mineral particles in the fabric, like that of non-plastic inclusions, may be an indication of forming methods (Velde and Druc 1993, 48–51). These attributes, however, may be difficult or impossible to observe in thin section.

VOIDS/PORES AND SURFACE TREATMENT

Ceramic fabrics also contain pores or voids that can be observed in thin section. The number, shape, and size of pores are either the result of the way in which the fabric has been prepared, or they occur due to the release of gas or shrinkage of clay during the drying and firing of the ceramic material (Velde and Druc 1999, 110–115; Reedy 2008, 191–193). Pores can also be indicative of the materials that were present during the preparation of a ceramic paste but were destroyed during the firing process (see above). The volume of pore space within the fabric, as well as the size and shape of pores, can affect the density, strength, permeability, and thermal resistance of the ceramic material and therefore can provide insight into its intended function (Shepard 1956, 125–126).

The examination of a ceramic thin section also can provide information about the ways in which the surface of the material has been treated. In turn, these aspects offer insight into the technology of manufacture and the development of stylistic trends. Details about the raw material constituents, structural nature, color, firing conditions, and thickness of glazes, slips, paints, and enamels can be ascertained (Reedy 2008, 194–206). The surface treatment of a ceramic material can indicate its function. Pottery, for example, may be decorated to hide flaws or signs of manufacture, and some treatments can enhance the impermeability of the material or make it easier to clean and handle (Velde and Druc 1999, 167).

Development of Aims and Sampling Strategy

A successful petrographic project should be developed with the aim of addressing a focused and sound archaeological problem. Thin-section analysis can be carried out on ceramic assemblages in order to answer a variety of questions, from the characterization or provenancing of a single ware or pottery type to a diachronic study of the ceramic material from an entire site or region. Without the formulation of such specific aims, the results of a petrographic thin-section analysis will have more limited archaeological meaning. It is crucial therefore to discuss these issues with a petrographer in the initial stages of the project. Collaboration with a petrographer will also allow for the development of a focused sampling strategy explicitly designed to meet the goals of the project. The objectives of the sampling strategy will vary according to the nature of the site and the assemblage under study, and they should be carefully planned, as they will determine the kind, quantity, and quality of interpretative data that is obtained. The availability of such resources as funding, labor, and time should also be taken into account as part of the planning process.

After a ceramic assemblage has been collected from the field, the sherds are cleaned and initially sorted by characteristics of the fabrics that are observable through macroscopic analysis, such as color, texture, surface finish, and visible inclusions. A general idea of the assemblage in terms of shapes, wares, and macroscopic fabrics will aid in the selection of samples, allow for the further development of analytical aims, and provide typological and other information that is valuable for interpretation. This examination can be performed either with the naked eye, or with the use of a hand lens or other means of low-level magnification. After fabrics have been broadly classified, a small selection of materials from each group is chosen for thin-section analysis. The type and the number of samples are decided according to the nature and complexity of the material, as well as the archaeological questions that are to be investigated. The samples must be representative of the assemblage in terms of shapes, wares, and macroscopic fabrics; a single, undiagnostic or unique sherd, for example, is unlikely to provide information that is meaningful to the assemblage as a whole. Furthermore, the samples should derive from well-stratified and securely dated contexts whenever possible, as the interpretation of results is enhanced when complemented by contextual information.

A sample for analysis is usually a small piece of pottery about 2–3 cm in size, but with special techniques, even smaller samples can be studied. Because the analytical technique is destructive, only those materials that have been thoroughly documented, photographed, and drawn should be submitted for study. A small, non-joining fragment from a nearly complete vessel is an ideal candidate for thin-section analysis because its microscopically determined data can be integrated with the information from the vase as a whole. The processes of thin-sectioning and examination are then carried out by the petrographer. Subsequently, the results of the petrographic analysis are combined with the typological, stratigraphic, and chronological study of the ceramics in order to provide a better understanding of the pottery on many levels.

Conclusion

The valuable information that is obtained through thin-section analysis can be combined with the results of other categories of investigation, such as analyses based on morphology, style, chronology, and function. Geological and ethnographic studies can also be carried out, such as the sampling and analysis of potential raw material sources and the examination of the methods of modern potters. Additionally, scientific techniques like x-ray diffraction, heavy mineral separation, and neutron activation analysis can also complement the technique by providing further information about the mineralogical and chemical composition of the ceramic fabric. When thin-section analysis is employed as part of a thorough, multi-disciplinary study of ceramic materials, it provides a wealth of additional interpretative data to the archaeologist, allowing for more accurate interpretations of the past, especially regarding pottery production, provenance, variations in technology over time and space, exchange networks on local and non-local scales, and even social issues such as choices of both manufacturers and consumers and traditions of manufacture.

Acknowledgments

The author is extremely grateful to the following individuals for the provision of valuable information and photographs: Peter M. Day, Eleanor Huffman, George H. Myer, Eleni Nodarou, Chronis Papanikolopoulos, and Elizabeth Shank.

Bibliography

Abbreviations follow the conventions suggested in the *American Journal of Archaeology* 111.1 (2007), pp. 14–34.

Bambauer, H.U., F. Taborszky, and H.D. Trochim. 1979. *Optical Determination of Rock-Forming Minerals*, by W.E. Tröger, Stuttgart.

Betancourt, P.P. 1984. *East Cretan White-on-Dark Ware: Studies on a Handmade Pottery of the Early to Middle Minoan Periods* (*University Museum Monograph* 51), Philadelphia.

Betancourt, P.P., T.K. Gaisser, E. Koss, R.F. Lyon, F.R. Matson, S. Montgomery, G.H. Myer, and C.P. Swann. 1979. *Vasilike Ware: An Early Bronze Age Pottery Style in Crete* (*SIMA* 56), Göteborg.

Braidwood, R.J., and L.S. Braidwood. 1960. *Excavations in the Plain of Antioch* I: *The Earlier Assemblages. Phases A–J* (*The University of Chicago Oriental Institute Publications* 61), Chicago.

Croft, W.J. 2006. *Under the Microscope: A Brief History of Microscopy* (*Series in Popular Science* 5), Hackensack, NJ.

Day, P.M. 1995. "Pottery Production and Consumption in the Sitia Bay Area during the New Palace Period," in *Achladia: Scavi e richerche della Missione greco-italiana in Creta orientale, 1991–1993*, M. Tsipopoulou and L. Vagnetti, eds., Rome, pp. 148–175.

———. 1997. "Ceramic Exchange between Towns and Outlying Settlements in Neopalatial East Crete," in *The Function of the "Minoan Villa." Proceedings of the Eighth International Symposium at the Swedish Institute in Athens, 6–8 June, 1992* (*SkrAth* 4°, 46), R. Hägg, ed., Stockholm, pp. 219–228.

Day, P.M., and V. Kilkoglou. 2001. "Analysis of Ceramics from the Kiln," in *A LM IA Ceramic Kiln in South-Central Crete: Function and Pottery Production* (*Hesperia Suppl.* 30), pp. 111–133.

Day, P.M., E. Kiriatzi, A. Tsolakidou, and V. Kilikoglou. 1999. "Group Therapy in Crete: A Comparison between Analyses by NAA and Thin Section Petrography of Early Minoan Pottery," *JAS* 26, pp. 1025–1036.

Day, P.M., and M. Relaki. 2003. "A Petrographic Analysis of the Neopalatial Pottery," in *Mochlos* IB: *Period III. Neopalatial Settlement on the Coast: The Artisans' Quarter and the Farmhouse at Chalinomouri. The Neopalatial Pottery* (*Prehistory Monographs* 8), K.A. Barnard and T.M. Brogan, eds., Philadelphia, pp. 13–32.

Day, P.M., and D.E. Wilson. 1998. "Consuming Power: Kamares Ware in Protopalatial Knossos," *Antiquity* 72, pp. 350–358.

Day, P.M., D.E. Wilson, and E. Kiriatzi. 1997. "Reassessing Specialization in Prepalatial Cretan Ceramic Production," in *TEXNH: Craftsmen, Craftswomen, and Craftsmanship in the Aegean Bronze Age. Proceedings of the Sixth International Aegean Conference, Philadelphia, Temple University, 18–21 April 1996* (*Aegaeum* 16), R. Laffineur and P.P. Betancourt, eds., Liège, pp. 275–289.

Deer, W.A., R.A. Howie, and J. Zussman. 1996. *An Introduction to Rock-Forming Minerals*, Essex, UK.

Doumas, Ch., ed. 1979. *Thera and the Aegean World* I. *Papers Presented at the Second International Scientific Congress, Santorini, Greece, August 1978*, London.

Einfalt, H.-C. 1979. "Chemical and Mineralogical Investigations of Sherds from the Akrotiri Excavations," in Doumas, ed., 1979, pp. 459–469.

Felts, W.M. 1942. "A Petrographic Examination of Potsherds from Ancient Troy," *AJA* 46, pp. 237–244.

Hardy, D.A., Ch. Doumas, J.A. Sakellarakis, and P.M. Warren, eds. 1990. *Thera and the Aegean World III. Proceedings of the Third International Congress, Santorini, Greece, 3–9 September 1989*. Volume I: *Archaeology*, London.

Humphries, D.W. 1992. *The Preparation of Thin Sections of Rocks, Minerals, and Ceramics* (*Microscopy Handbooks* 24), Oxford.

Jones, R.E. 1986. *Greek and Cypriot Pottery: A Review of Scientific Studies* (*The British School at Athens Fitch Laboratory Occasional Paper* 1), Athens.

Lepsius, G.R. 1890. *Greichische Marmorstudien*, Berlin.

Matson, F.R. 1942. "Technological Ceramic Studies," *College Art Journal* 1, pp. 25–28.

―――. 1945. "Technological Development of Pottery in Northern Syria during the Chalcolithic Age," *Journal of the American Ceramic Society* 28, pp. 20–25.

―――. 1965. "Ceramic Ecology: An Approach to the Study of Early Cultures of the Near East," in *Ceramics and Man*, F.R. Matson, ed., Chicago, pp. 202–217.

―――. 1972. "Ceramic Studies," in *The Minnesota Messenia Expedition: Reconstructing a Bronze Age Regional Environment*, W.A. McDonald and G.R. Rapp, Jr., eds., Minneapolis, pp. 200–224.

Matthers, J., ed. 1981. *The River Qoueiq, Northern Syria, and its Catchment* II (*BAR-IS* 98), Oxford.

Moltesen, M. 1994. *The Lepsius Marble Samples*, Copenhagen.

Myer, G.H., and P.P. Betancourt. 1981. "The Composition of Vasilike Ware and the Production of the Mottled Colors of the Slip," in *Scientific Studies in Ancient Ceramics* (*BMOP* 19), M.J. Hughes, ed., pp. 51–55.

————. 1990. "The Fabrics at Kommos," in *Kommos* II: *The Final Neolithic through Middle Minoan III Pottery*, P.P. Betancourt, Princeton, pp. 1–13.

Myer, G.H., K.G. McIntosh, and P.P. Betancourt. 1995. "Definition of Pottery Fabrics by Ceramic Petrography," in *Pseira* I: *The Minoan Buildings on the West Side of Area A* (*University Museum Monographs* 94), P.P. Betancourt and C. Davaras, eds., Philadelphia, pp. 143–153.

Nesse, W.D. 2004. *Introduction to Optical Mineralogy*, 3rd ed., Oxford.

Noll, W. 1979. "Material and Techniques of the Minoan Ceramics of Thera and Crete," in Doumas, ed., 1979, pp. 493–505.

Orton, T., P. Tyers, and A. Vince. 1993. *Pottery in Archaeology*, Cambridge.

Peacock, D.P.S. 1968. "A Petrological Study of Certain Iron Age Pottery from Western England," *Proceedings of the Prehistoric Society* 34, pp. 414–427.

————. 1971. "Petrography of Certain Coarse Pottery," in *Excavations at Fishbourne 1961–1969*. Volume II: *The Finds* (*Reports of the Research Committee of the Society of Antiquaries of London* 27), B. Cunliffe, ed., Leeds, pp. 255–259.

Reedy, C.L. 2008. *Thin-Section Petrography of Stone and Ceramic Cultural Materials*, Plymouth, UK.

Riley, J.A. 1979. "The Petrological Investigation of Roman and Islamic Ceramics from Cyrenaica," *Libyan Studies* 10, pp. 35–46.

————.1981a. "The Late Bronze Age Aegean and the Roman Mediterranean: A Case for Comparison," in *Production and Distribution: A Ceramic Viewpoint* (*BAR-IS* 120), H. Howard and E.L. Morris, eds., Oxford, pp. 133–143.

————. 1981b. "Petrological Examination of Bronze Age IV Fabrics," in Matthers, ed., 1981, pp. 349–361.

————. 1981c. "Petrological Examination of Coarse-Ware Stirrup-Jars from Mycenae," *BSA* 76, pp. 335–340.

————. 1981d. "Petrological Examination of Two Mycenaean Sherds," in Matthers, ed., 1981, pp. 413–415.

————. 1982. "The Petrological Analysis of Aegean Ceramics," in *Current Research in Ceramics: Thin Section Studies* (*BMOP* 32), I. Freestone, C. Johns, and T. Potter, eds., pp. 1–7.

————.1983. "The Contribution of Ceramic Petrology to Our Understanding of Minoan Society," in *Minoan Society. Proceedings of the Cambridge Colloquium 1981*, O. Krzyszkowska and L. Nixon, eds., Bristol, pp. 283–292.

Riley, J.A., D.P.S. Peacock, and A.C. Renfrew. 1980. "The Petrological Characterization of Ceramics from Knossos and Mycenae," *Revue d'Archéometrie* 3, pp. 245–250.

Roux, V., and M.A. Courty. 1998. "Identification of Wheel-Fashioning Methods: Technological Analysis of 4th–3rd Millennium B.C. Oriental Ceramics," *JAS* 25, pp. 747–763.

Shepard, A.O. 1942. *Rio Grande Glaze Paint Ware: A Study Illustrating the Place of Ceramic Technological Analysis in Archaeological Research* (*Carnegie Institution of Washington Publication* 528), Washington, D.C.

——. 1956. *Ceramics for the Archaeologist*, Washington, D.C.

——. 1965. "Rio Grande Glaze-Paint Pottery: A Test of Petrographic Analysis," in *Ceramics and Man*, F.R. Matson, ed., Chicago, pp. 62–87.

Shriner, C., and M.J. Dorais. 1999. "A Comparative Electron Microprobe Study of Lerna III and IV Ceramics and Local Clay-Rich Sediments," *Archaeometry* 41, pp. 25–49.

Shriner, C., and H.H. Murray. 2001. "Explaining Sudden Ceramic Change at Early Helladic Lerna: A Technological Paradigm," in *Archaeology and Clays* (*BAR-IS* 942), I.C. Druc, ed., pp. 1–17.

Sorby, H.C. 1851. "On the Microscopical Structure of the Calcareous Grit of the Yorkshire Coast," *The Quarterly Journal of the Geological Society of London* 7, pp. 1–6.

——. 1882. "Preparation of Transparent Sections of Rocks and Minerals," *The Northern Microscopist* 17, pp. 101–106, 133–140.

Vaughan, S.J. 1990. "Petrographic Analysis of the Early Cycladic Wares from Akrotiri, Thera," in Hardy et al., eds., 1990, pp. 470–487.

——. 1991a. "Late Cypriot Base Ring Ware: Studies in Raw Materials and Technology," in *Recent Developments in Ceramic Petrology* (*BMOP* 81), A. Middleton and I. Freestone, eds., pp. 337–368.

——. 1991b. "Material and Technical Characterization of Base Ring Ware: A New Fabric Typology," in *Cypriot Ceramics: Reading the Prehistoric Record* (*University Museum Monographs* 74), J.A. Barlow, D.L. Bolger, and B. Kling, eds., Philadelphia, pp. 119–130.

Velde, B., and I.C. Druc. 1999. *Archaeological Ceramic Materials*, Berlin.

Williams, D.F. 1979a. "Ceramic Petrology and the Archaeologist," in *Pottery and the Archaeologist*, M. Millet, ed., London, pp. 73–75.

——. 1979b. "A Petrological Examination of Pottery from Thera," in Doumas, ed., 1979, pp. 507–514.

Whitbread, I.K. 1986. "The Characterization of Argillaceous Inclusions in Ceramic Thin Sections," *Archaeometry* 28, pp. 79–88.

——. 1989. "A Proposal for the Systematic Description of Thin Sections Towards the Study of Ancient Ceramic Technology," in *Archaeometry. Proceedings of the 25th International Symposium*, Y. Maniatis, ed., Amsterdam, pp. 127–138.

——. 1996. "Detection and Interpretation of Preferred Orientation in Ceramic Thin Sections," in *Imaging the Past* (*BMOP* 114), T. Higgins, P. Main, and J. Long, eds., London, pp. 173–181.

Woods, A.J. 1985. "An Introductory Note on the Use of Tangential Thin Sections for Distinguishing Between Wheel-Thrown and Coil/Ring-Built Vessels," *Bulletin of the Experimental Firing Group* 3, pp. 100–114.